English for Listening, Speaking, Reading & Writing

NEW CONNECTION

BRING YOUR ENGLISH TO THE NEXT LEVEL

WORKBOOK 1

UNIT 1

Just for Fun

Words

Track 01

Listen to the audio. Match the pictures with the words or phrases you hear.

1.

a 

b 

c 

2.

a 

b 

c 

Conversation

A. Complete the Dialogue

Choose the answers.

1. **A:** Do you have any hobbies? **B:** ______________________
   a. No, I don't swim. **b.** Yes. I love to paint. **c.** I'm free now.

2. **A:** That's cool. I like playing sports. **B:** ______________________
   a. Do you play baseball? **b.** We can practice together. **c.** How good are you at chess?

3. **A:** It's one of my favorite sports. **B:** ______________________
   a. We can go swimming. **b.** Great. Can you teach me? **c.** I like painting too.

B. Comprehension

Track 02

Listen to the dialogue. Choose the answers.

1. What is Ernest's hobby?
   a. painting **b.** playing chess **c.** swimming **d.** reading

2. What hobby do Nicole and Ernest share?
   a. playing basketball **b.** swimming **c.** playing guitar **d.** cooking

3. What is NOT one of Nicole's hobbies?
   a. painting **b.** playing video games **c.** playing sports **d.** reading comic books

Unit Test

Grammar

Use the correct form of the words to complete the sentences. Use contractions if possible.

eat	drive	worry	not cook	catch	study

1. Sam ________________ his kids to school every morning.
2. I ________________ very much. I often ________________ at restaurants.
3. That baseball player always ________________ the ball.
4. Terry ________________ French in university.
5. Emily's parents often ________________ about her.

Reading

A. Fill in the Blanks

Use the correct form of the words to complete the sentences.

hobby	improve	think	active	interest

1. He has a(n) ________________ life, and is always busy.
2. He goes fishing on weekends. It's one of his ________________.
3. Mike wants to ________________ his basketball skills. He practices every day.
4. My sister has a great ________________ in singing. She really loves it.
5. It's too noisy here. I can't ________________.

B. Comprehension Track 03

*Listen to the article. Check **True** or **False**.*

	True	False
1. People with hobbies are healthier.	☐	☐
2. Puzzles keep your body active.	☐	☐
3. It is best to have just one hobby.	☐	☐
4. Hobbies are a good way to meet friends.	☐	☐
5. There are only a few hobby clubs.	☐	☐

Listening Questions

Best Response Questions

Track 04

Listen to the question or statement and choose the best response.

1. **a.** I am great at football. **b.** I play every Saturday. **c.** I play football on the school team.
2. **a.** Yes, he has a hobby. **b.** Yes, he likes to go to the gym. **c.** No, he never does.
3. **a.** Yes, he can't play. **b.** No, Max can play. **c.** Yes, he is able to play.
4. **a.** with my dad **b.** on Friday evenings **c.** at the lake near my house
5. **a.** Yes. I often go on weekends. **b.** What time should we go? **c.** The movies are interesting.
6. **a.** She has many hobbies. **b.** She enjoys going to the park. **c.** She likes being in the water.
7. **a.** I sometimes play basketball. **b.** I don't collect coins. **c.** I work at a big company.

Conversation

Track 05

Listen to each conversation and answer the question.

1. **a.** He doesn't dance often. **b.** He never dances. **c.** He dances every day.
2. **a.** eighteen **b.** seventeen **c.** nineteen
3. **a.** She is very busy. **b.** She is not busy. **c.** He doesn't need to pay any money.

Reading Questions

Vocabulary and Grammar

Choose the best answer to fill in each blank.

1. He likes to use his brain. He enjoys ________________.
   a. to read　**b.** swimming　**c.** playing chess　**d.** cook

2. Mark exercises often. He goes to ________________ almost every day.
   a. the movies　**b.** the gym　**c.** the school　**d.** a sport

3. They go to the bookstore to ________________.
   a. read comics　**b.** play tennis　**c.** watch TV　**d.** see plays

4. Mary ________________ great pictures. This one is beautiful!
   a. shops　**b.** practices　**c.** climbs　**d.** paints

5. The children ________________ for school at 7:30 every morning.
   a. leaves　**b.** leaving　**c.** leave　**d.** to leave

6. ________________ your boyfriend want to come with us?
   a. Do　**b.** Don't　**c.** Does　**d.** Is

7. ________________ do you like this guy? He is not a nice person.
   a. How　**b.** What　**c.** When　**d.** Why

Cloze

Choose the best answer to fill in each blank.

Hobbies are fun and interesting. They may also make people healthier. Some hobbies, like chess and puzzles, are good for the **1.** ________________. Other hobbies help you stay healthy. Swimming and basketball keep your body **2.** ________________. Hobbies are a great way to meet people too. People with friends are often healthier than people without friends. There are many clubs for different hobbies. People in the club easily become friends **3.** ________________ they like the same things. Hobbies can help you in many ways. Get a hobby!

1. **a.** heart　**b.** interest　**c.** brain　**d.** body

2. **a.** active　**b.** afraid　**c.** safe　**d.** fun

3. **a.** so　**b.** because　**c.** after　**d.** and

UNIT 2 Grocery Shopping

Words Track 06

Listen to the audio. Match the pictures with the words you hear.

1\.

a 

b 

c 

2\.

a 

b 

c 

Conversation

A. Matching

Match the sentences.

a. It's right here. I can get it.	**b.** OK. The candy section is over there.
c. I want some toast and jam.	**d.** We need a bottle of juice and some onions.

1. **A:** What should we buy? **B:** ____________________
2. **A:** What would you like for breakfast? **B:** ____________________
3. **A:** I also want a chocolate bar. **B:** ____________________
4. **A:** Where's the cheese? **B:** ____________________

B. Comprehension Track 07

*Listen to the dialogue. Check **True** or **False**.*

	True	False
1. Esther and Joanne are at the mall.	☐	☐
2. Esther and Joanne buy toilet paper first.	☐	☐
3. Joanne already has cheese.	☐	☐
4. Joanne can't carry the water. It's too heavy.	☐	☐
5. Esther doesn't want to have chocolate.	☐	☐

Unit Test

Grammar

Choose the answers.

1. How ________________ milk do we have?
   a. many　**b.** a few　**c.** much　**d.** any
2. I want to eat ________________ sandwich.
   a. a　**b.** some　**c.** a lot of　**d.** an
3. They would like ________________ hamburgers.
   a. much　**b.** a little　**c.** any　**d.** two
4. Ella loves honey. She puts ________________ it in her tea.
   a. any　**b.** some　**c.** a little　**d.** a lot of
5. I need to lose weight, so I don't want ________________ dessert.
   a. any　**b.** some　**c.** a few　**d.** many
6. There are ________________ men in the room.
   a. a　**b.** some　**c.** a little　**d.** any

Reading

A. Fill in the Blanks

Use the correct form of the words to complete the sentences.

delicious	meaning	important	wedding	snack

1. This is a really ________________ apple. It's sweet and juicy.
2. Remember to bring a gift to their ________________.
3. The president is a(n) ________________ person.
4. The dinner is not ready. Do you want to have a(n) ________________ first?
5. This word has a lot of different ________________.

B. Comprehension Track 08

Listen to the article. Check ***True*** *or* ***False****.*

	True	False
1. Fruits have many interesting meanings in different countries.	☐	☐
2. The Greeks think that apples mean peace.	☐	☐
3. Apples are a sign of love to Chinese people.	☐	☐
4. In English culture, cherries bring good luck.	☐	☐

Listening Questions

Best Response Questions

Track 09

Listen to the question or statement and choose the best response.

1. **a.** Yes, there are. **b.** Yes. I usually go to the supermarket. **c.** No. We should buy some.
2. **a.** I'm not sure. Check the drawer. **b.** Are your hands dirty? **c.** Of course. It smells good.
3. **a.** I have $5. **b.** It is $1.50. **c.** I need four of them.
4. **a.** Yes, we have two. **b.** Yes. We don't have any at home. **c.** Yes, I also like them.
5. **a.** I go to the convenience store. **b.** I usually drive there. **c.** I like to go to the gym.
6. **a.** No. We just need some bread. **b.** Yes, it's not on the list. **c.** I can get the onions.
7. **a.** We need to go shopping. **b.** Yes, we need a lot. **c.** We should get some cheese.

Conversation

Track 10

Listen to each conversation and answer the question.

1. **a.** some fruit **b.** a piece of paper **c.** groceries
2. **a.** wash his hands **b.** order dessert **c.** give money
3. **a.** take her books **b.** give her the books **c.** buy her some books

Reading Questions

Vocabulary and Grammar

Choose the best answer to fill in each blank.

1. You can clean the floor with this ________________.
   a. drawer **b.** toilet **c.** basket **d.** mop
2. We have to buy some jam. Do we need anything ________________?
   a. to buy **b.** also **c.** else **d.** there
3. I have a ________________ at my office. I use it after lunch.
   a. doughnut **b.** section **c.** list **d.** toothbrush
4. I'm thirsty. Could I get ________________ cup of water?
   a. an **b.** a **c.** the **d.** a few
5. He puts ________________ sugar in his coffee.
   a. a few **b.** any **c.** a lot of **d.** many
6. ________________ teacher is sick today.
   a. Any **b.** These **c.** The **d.** Little
7. Can you buy some ________________ before you come home?
   a. soap **b.** tomato **c.** sandwich **d.** chocolate bar

Cloze

Choose the best answer to fill in each blank.

Fruits are good to eat, but they also have many **1.** ________________. For example, apples are a special fruit in different cultures. In Greek stories, apples are a sign of love and beauty. Apples also give the Norse gods long life. In Chinese culture, apples bring peace. Pomegranates are a(n) **2.** ________________ fruit too. In Greece, friends bring pomegranates to weddings for good luck. Pomegranates mean lots of children in China because of their many seeds. Fruits are not just a healthy **3.** ________________. They are a lot more than that.

1. **a.** mean **b.** meanings **c.** means **d.** meaning
2. **a.** healthy **b.** delicious **c.** natural **d.** important
3. **a.** vegetable **b.** fast food **c.** grocery **d.** snack

UNIT 3

Blue Skies

Words

Track 11

Listen to the audio. Match the pictures with the words you hear.

1.

a

b
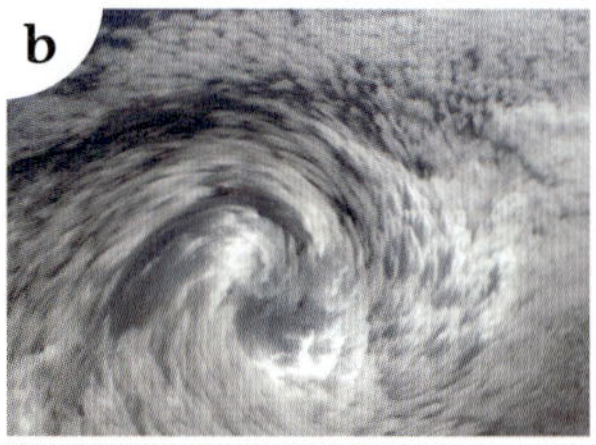

c
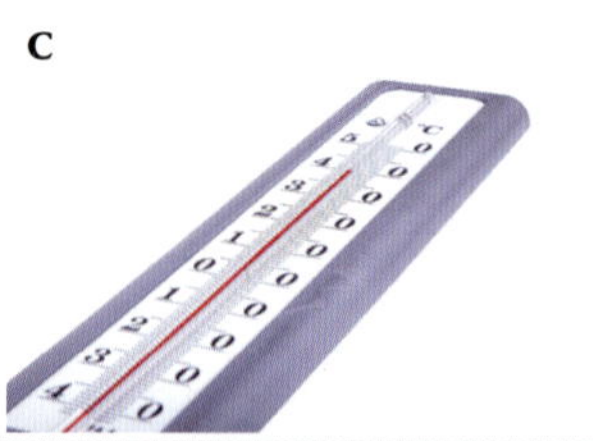

2.

a

b
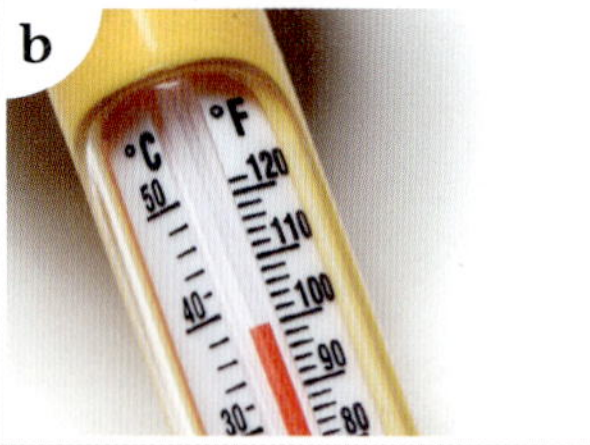

c

Conversation

A. Complete the Dialogue

Choose the answers.

1. **A:** What's your favorite type of weather? **B:** ____________________
   a. No, it doesn't snow here. **b.** You can see rainbows. **c.** I love rainy days.

2. **A:** It never rains in Arizona. **B:** ____________________
   a. You should carry an umbrella. **b.** The winter is warmer. **c.** Is it dry all year round?

3. **A:** Almost. I prefer desert weather. **B:** ____________________
   a. I am from California. **b.** That sounds too hot for me. **c.** It's the same here.

B. Comprehension

Track 12

Listen to the dialogue. Choose the answers.

1. Where does Henry come from?
   a. He's from New York. **b.** He's from Ethiopia.
   c. He's from Australia. **d.** He's from California.

2. What kind of weather does Lizzy like?
   a. She likes hot weather. **b.** She likes rainy weather.
   c. She likes snowy weather. **d.** She likes windy days.

Unit Test

Grammar

Use the correct form of the words to complete the sentences. Some blanks may have more than one possible answer.

1. **A:** Why do you prefer the red car?
   B: It seems ________________ (fast) than the other cars.
2. **A:** I often go to the pizza place.
   B: Me too. It is the ________________ (good) restaurant in the area!
3. **A:** Do you like his mom?
   B: Yes. His mom is ________________ (friendly) than his dad.
4. **A:** Could you be ________________ (quiet)?
   B: OK. I am sorry.
5. **A:** The temperature in Antarctica can reach minus 89 degrees Celsius.
   B: Yeah. It is the ________________ (cold) place on earth.

Reading

A. Fill in the Blanks

Use the correct form of the words to complete the sentences.

sunny	dry	rain	low	speed

1. The plants look ________________. They need some water.
2. The car goes at a ________________ of 80 kilometers per hour.
3. The cost of living is ________________ in the small town.
4. We want to go to the beach on a ________________ day.
5. There is no ________________, so you don't need an umbrella.

B. Comprehension Track 13

*Listen to the article. Check **True** or **False**.*

	True	False
1. Yuma, Arizona is the driest place on earth.	☐	☐
2. Lloró, Colombia gets a lot of rain.	☐	☐
3. It is not very wet in Antarctica.	☐	☐
4. Typhoons need cold air and rain.	☐	☐
5. The Philippines gets seven or eight typhoons a month.	☐	☐

Listening Questions

Best Response Questions

Track 14

Listen to the question or statement and choose the best response.

1. **a.** I prefer rainy days. **b.** My favorite season is summer. **c.** It is snowy now.
2. **a.** Yes, it's really dry. **b.** No. It's a beautiful day. **c.** It's a windy season.
3. **a.** Luckily, there is a lot of snow. **b.** Alright. The weather is great! **c.** Sounds good. The wind is very strong.
4. **a.** It's quite hot in summer. **b.** Cloudy days are the best. **c.** My favorite weather is rain.
5. **a.** I really like the spring. **b.** Yes. The temperatures there are low. **c.** No. It is always cold.
6. **a.** I don't like the summer. **b.** I like the fall best. **c.** Today is a lovely day.
7. **a.** It's warm enough here. **b.** No way! It's too cold outside. **c.** The weather is too nice to play.

Conversation

Track 15

Listen to each conversation and answer the question.

1. **a.** The woman needs a new sofa. **b.** His sofa is like hers. **c.** He wants to sit down.
2. **a.** He isn't sure. **b.** No, he doesn't. **c.** Yes, he does.
3. **a.** It is hot most of the time. **b.** It is hot sometimes. **c.** It is never hot.

Reading Questions

Vocabulary and Grammar

Choose the best answer to fill in each blank.

1. Don't let the ________________ blow your hat away.
   a. rainbow **b.** fog **c.** cloud **d.** wind

2. I don't like candy. I ________________ fruit to candy.
   a. prefer **b.** choose **c.** like **d.** eat

3. It's 25 ________________ outside. The weather is perfect!
   a. degrees **b.** meters **c.** temperature **d.** heat

4. By Christmas, the ground is usually covered in ________________.
   a. typhoons **b.** rain **c.** snow **d.** storms

5. Raymond is my ________________ friend. We have many common interests.
   a. less **b.** better **c.** best **d.** most

6. Her house is ________________ to the office than mine.
   a. closer **b.** closed **c.** closest **d.** close

7. His dog is the most ________________ dog in the world.
   a. more friendly **b.** friendly **c.** friendlier **d.** friendliest

Cloze

Choose the best answer to fill in each blank.

Weather is different all over the world. The sunniest place on earth is Yuma, Arizona. It is sunny for 4,050 hours every year, and most days have around 11 hours of sun. It can be very hot. The temperature can go **1.** ________________ 50 degrees Celsius. The wettest place in the world is Lloro, Colombia. It gets 13,290 millimeters of rain a year. The world's driest place is also the coldest place. It is Antarctica. Antarctica's **2.** ________________ can go down to minus 89 degrees Celsius. It is **3.** ________________ than any other place in the world too. The winds can be strong like a typhoon!

1. **a.** as high **b.** around **c.** up to **d.** hottest
2. **a.** temperature **b.** ice **c.** climate **d.** storm
3. **a.** more wind **b.** windier **c.** windy **d.** windiest

UNIT 4

The World of Computers

Words Track 16

Listen and match the audio with the phrases.

1. a listen to music | b surf the Internet | c talk to friends

2. a watch videos | b look at pictures | c read the news

Conversation

A. Matching

Match the sentences.

a. You're the best! Thanks a lot!	**b.** There's a problem with my phone.
c. That's OK. I can take it to a store.	**d.** I have to type up a report.

1. A: Is something wrong?
   B: ____________________
2. A: Why do you need your computer?
   B: ____________________
3. A: Sorry. I am not able to fix it.
   B: ____________________
4. A: You can always use my computer.
   B: ____________________

B. Comprehension Track 17

*Listen to the dialogue. Check **True** or **False**.*

	True	False
1. Sara wants to watch videos on the Internet.	☐	☐
2. Sara needs to finish her homework.	☐	☐
3. Ken knows a lot about computers.	☐	☐
4. Ken can fix Sara's computer quickly.	☐	☐
5. Sara would like Ken to go to the computer store with.	☐	☐

Grammar

Choose the answers.

1. She wants to go to college, ________________ she doesn't have enough money.
   a. so **b.** and **c.** or **d.** but

2. We can ride the train ________________ take the bus.
   a. and **b.** or **c.** though **d.** but

3. The guitar ________________ good when he plays it.
   a. smells **b.** feels **c.** looks **d.** sounds

4. Give her some bread ________________ milk.
   a. when **b.** but **c.** and **d.** taste

Reading

A. Fill in the Blanks

Use the correct form of the words to complete the sentences.

Internet	smartphone	game	access	train

1. Only the members can ________________ to the club.
2. She likes to play computer ________________.
3. Students are not allowed to use their ________________ during the class.
4. We can buy shoes on the ________________.
5. I get to work by ________________.

B. Comprehension Track 18

Listen to the article. Choose the answers.

1. What is the Internet on a smartphone called?
   a. Mobile Internet **b.** Telephone Internet **c.** Pocket Internet **d.** Internet to go

2. What can't people do with their smartphones?
   a. play mobile games **b.** check e-mails **c.** use SNS **d.** catch a bus

3. Which is true?
   a. People can do many things with their smartphones.
   b. People should stay at home to use the Mobile Internet.
   c. Children can't use the smartphone before they could speak in full sentences.
   d. Less and less people use smartphones these days.

Listening Questions

Best Response Questions

Track 19

Listen to the question or statement and choose the best response.

1. **a.** No. I prefer to read a newspaper. **b.** Yes. I use my computer often. **c.** I usually write it by hand.
2. **a.** I need to get a new one. **b.** I send e-mails and watch videos. **c.** I use it four hours a day.
3. **a.** Yes, it's very slow. **b.** I have my own computer. **c.** Yes, it works fine.
4. **a.** Yes. I like to look at pictures. **b.** Yes. I can find anything on the Internet. **c.** That's right. The information is correct.
5. **a.** Sure. I can give you a call. **b.** Maybe. What's the problem with it? **c.** OK. Does it work well?
6. **a.** He uses it to type up reports. **b.** He can type very fast. **c.** He shares one with his roommate.
7. **a.** Yes. She wants to own a computer. **b.** Yes. This one is hers. **c.** Yes. She uses my computer.

Conversation

Track 20

Listen to each conversation and answer the question.

1. **a.** The TV doesn't work. **b.** Mona's TV is old. **c.** Mona doesn't have a TV.
2. **a.** He must do some work. **b.** He feels worried about it. **c.** He doesn't feel well.
3. **a.** She wants to run too. **b.** She has an idea. **c.** She doesn't like running.

Reading Questions

Vocabulary and Grammar

Choose the best answer to fill in each blank.

1. Can you turn ________________ the radio? There's a good show at six p.m.
   a. on **b.** out **c.** down **d.** off

2. Do you know that ________________? Who is she?
   a. people **b.** store **c.** guy **d.** person

3. Meg has ________________ of friends. Everybody likes her.
   a. many **b.** a lot **c.** a few **d.** much

4. I want to buy this camera, ________________ it costs too much.
   a. or **b.** but **c.** and **d.** neither

5. Michelle ________________ sick. Can you take her to the hospital?
   a. needs **b.** tastes **c.** feels **d.** smells

6. This painting looks ________________!
   a. beauty **b.** beautifully **c.** not beautiful **d.** beautiful

7. That sounds ________________ a dog.
   a. alike **b.** likely **c.** likes **d.** like

Cloze

Choose the best answer to fill in each blank.

Today, the Internet is everywhere! With **1.** ________________, you can carry the Internet in your pocket. This is called the Mobile Internet. People use it to check e-mails, use Facebook, and play games. You can **2.** ________________ the Internet with your smartphones at any place. You don't have to be at home or at work. You can use the Internet on public transportation like a bus or a train. According to the survey, more than 1.76 billion people around the world have a smartphone. Even some **3.** ________________ under two who can't speak in full sentences have used a smartphone!

1. **a.** computers **b.** TVs **c.** radios **d.** smartphones

2. **a.** access **b.** talk to **c.** deny **d.** watch

3. **a.** workers **b.** adults **c.** dogs **d.** children

UNIT 5 Man's Best Friends

Words Track 21

Listen to the audio. Match the pictures with the words you hear.

1. a  b  c 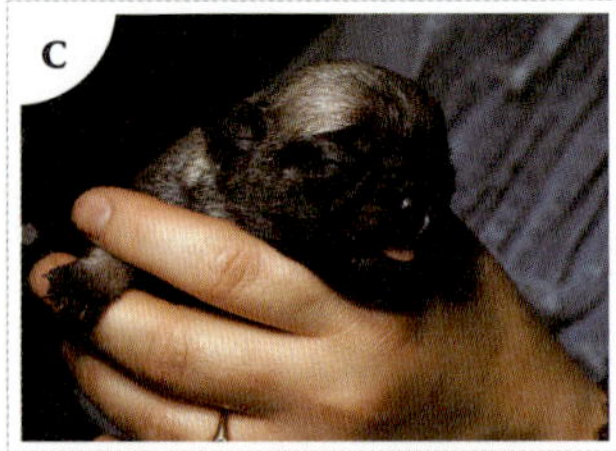

2. a  b 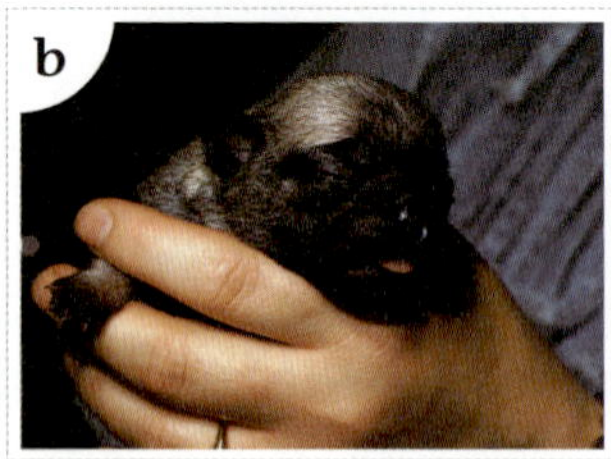 c 

Conversation

A. Complete the Dialogue

Choose the answers.

1. **A:** This is my new puppy **B:** ______________________
   a. Wow. I love snakes! **b.** Cool. I want a pet, but my apartment is too small. **c.** Yeah, we should look at cats.

2. **A:** Why don't you get a bird? **B:** ______________________
   a. A puppy sounds great. **b.** I don't like to keep animals in cages. **c.** I don't have a yard.

3. **A:** Then you should get a cat. **B:** ______________________
   a. I can't get an elephant or a panda. **b.** You should train your cat. **c.** That sounds like a good idea.

B. Comprehension Track 22

Listen to the dialogue. Choose the answers.

1. What kind of pet does Hugh have?
   a. a dog **b.** a cat **c.** a fish **d.** a snake

2. Why can't Penelope have a pet?
   a. Her apartment is not big enough. **b.** She does not like animals.
   c. It's too much work for her. **d.** Her place does not allow pets.

Grammar

Use the correct form of the words to complete the sentences. Some blanks may have more than one possible answer.

travel	buy	have	listen	finish	play

1. He is hungry. He wants ________________ lunch now.
2. She loves ________________ to rock music.
3. He knows a lot about ________________ football.
4. ________________ is a good way to meet new friends. You can talk to people from different countries.
5. We hope ________________ our work soon.
6. Their plan is ________________ a bigger house next year.

Reading

A. Fill in the Blanks

Use the correct form of the words to complete the sentences.

hippo	understand	wild	yard	furniture

1. ________________ animals are dangerous.
2. The cat is outside in the ________________.
3. My dog ________________ me. He is just like a family member.
4. A ________________ is a very big animal. It likes to stay in water.
5. We need some office ________________, like computer desks and chairs.

B. Comprehension Track 23

Listen to the article. Check ***True*** *or* ***False****.*

	True	False
1. Jessica is a teenager.	☐	☐
2. Jessica can understand some English.	☐	☐
3. The Jouberts give Jessica coffee.	☐	☐
4. Jessica stays away from other hippos.	☐	☐
5. Hippos look nice, but they can hurt people.	☐	☐

Listening Questions

Best Response Questions

Track 24

Listen to the question or statement and choose the best response.

1. **a.** They live a long time. **b.** I keep two cats at home. **c.** I really like dogs.
2. **a.** He can be very naughty sometimes. **b.** He likes to eat fish and vegetables. **c.** He really likes you.
3. **a.** No, I'm scared of snakes. **b.** Yes, I have a pet snake. **c.** Yes. It takes a lot of hard work.
4. **a.** I enjoy walking her. **b.** I want to get one soon. **c.** She is one year old.
5. **a.** She is in my bedroom. **b.** She is called Tikki. **c.** She can sing and say a few words.
6. **a.** Yes. I don't have any. **b.** Yes. You can bring him home. **c.** Yes. I love animals.
7. **a.** He stays inside the house. **b.** He is easy to care for. **c.** He can open the doors.

Conversation

Track 25

Listen to each conversation and answer the question.

1. **a.** It is a boy. **b.** It can be mean. **c.** It is a girl.
2. **a.** The woman should teach her dog. **b.** The woman needs an older dog. **c.** The woman should give away her dog.
3. **a.** something to eat **b.** something to play with **c.** something to wear

Reading Questions

Vocabulary and Grammar

Choose the best answer to fill in each blank.

1. A dog can have as many as 12 ________________ at one time.
   a. kittens **b.** pets **c.** rabbits **d.** puppies

2. She feeds mice to her ________________.
   a. bird **b.** fish **c.** snake **d.** panda

3. I don't like zoos. Animals shouldn't live in ________________.
   a. forests **b.** apartments **c.** cages **d.** yards

4. I need to send an e-mail ________________ my sister.
   a. through **b.** to **c.** for **d.** X

5. Her favorite activity is ________________ movies.
   a. watched **b.** watches **c.** watch **d.** watching

6. Is it true? Do you really want to quit ________________ to school?
   a. to go **b.** to going **c.** go **d.** going

7. They want ________________ the address of the restaurant.
   a. knowing **b.** knew **c.** to know **d.** know

Cloze

Choose the best answer to fill in each blank.

Jessica is Tonie and Shirley Joubert's pet. They raise her like their own daughter. Many people keep pets, but Jessica is special. She is a 1,000-kilogram hippo. Jessica can **1.** ________________ a few words of English, and she drinks 20 liters of coffee a day. She spends most of her day **2.** ________________ in the river, but she always comes home for dinner. Tonie tries to keep Jessica in the yard, but it is hard to keep out a giant hippo. Jessica often damages **3.** ________________ in the house. The Jouberts have to fix their beds and chairs a lot. Jessica really is a strange pet!

1. **a.** listen **b.** treat **c.** repeat **d.** understand

2. **a.** swimming **b.** swims **c.** to swim **d.** to swimming

3. **a.** furniture **b.** machines **c.** clothes **d.** people

UNIT 6 At the Department Store

Words

Track 26

Listen to the audio. Match the pictures with the words or phrases you hear.

1.

a

b

c

2.

a

b

c

Conversation

A. Matching

Match the sentences.

a. First, walk straight. Then turn left at the light.	**b.** Yeah. It tastes terrible.
c. They are near the hats, on the left.	**d.** No problem.

1. **A:** Excuse me. Where are the jackets? **B:** ____________________
2. **A:** Thank you so much! **B:** ____________________
3. **A:** How can I get to the bank? **B:** ____________________
4. **A:** Oh man! I don't like this soup. **B:** ____________________

B. Comprehension

Track 27

*Listen to the dialogue. Check **True** or **False**.*

	True	False
1. The two men are in a night market.	☐	☐
2. The clerk is near the baseball caps.	☐	☐
3. The clerk tells the men to go straight and turn right at the T-shirts.	☐	☐
4. The two men walk upstairs to find the baseball caps.	☐	☐
5. They plan to eat something later.	☐	☐

Grammar

Choose the answers.

1. ________________ the milk tea. It's delicious.
   a. Trying **b.** To try **c.** Should try **d.** Try
2. Good morning, students. Please ________________ your books to page 221.
   a. opening **b.** open **c.** opens **d.** to opening
3. I'm really tired. ________________ go to the party tonight.
   a. Let's not **b.** Not **c.** Never **d.** Let not
4. It's very cold today, so ________________ a warm coat.
   a. be bringing **b.** bring **c.** bringing **d.** does bring
5. You should be quiet in the library. ________________ so loudly!
   a. Talk **b.** Let's talk **c.** Don't talk **d.** No talk

Reading

A. Fill in the Blanks

Use the correct form of the words to complete the sentences.

mean	story	space	ice-skate	serve

1. I love this place. It ________________ great food.
2. Jenny's apartment building has 20 ________________.
3. Ted plays hockey, so he can ________________ very well.
4. The name Peter ________________ "rock."
5. The classroom has enough ________________ for 50 students.

B. Comprehension Track 28

*Listen to the article. Check **True** or **False**.*

	True	False
1. Centum City is in Seoul, South Korea.	☐	☐
2. Over 6,000 people work in Macy's Department Store.	☐	☐
3. The Shinsegae has a roof garden and a golf course.	☐	☐
4. Cine de Chef is a new type of department store.	☐	☐
5. You can get to Centum City only by bus.	☐	☐

Listening Questions

Best Response Questions

Track 29

Listen to the question or statement and choose the best response.

1. **a.** No. He looks very tired. **b.** Yes. He's next to the stairs. **c.** No. He's just there.
2. **a.** I'm sorry. I have no idea. **b.** The police officer is in his car. **c.** Go straight. You can find them there.
3. **a.** Turn right. It's on the second floor. **b.** It's on the right side. You should cross the road. **c.** Yes, it's on the left side of the road.
4. **a.** Yes, it's down the street. **b.** Yes, it's inside the department store. **c.** Yes. You can find it in the basement.
5. **a.** No, I'm not from around here. **b.** Yes, I need some directions. **c.** It's over there, beside that park.
6. **a.** Let's go to the men's department. **b.** It's on the first floor. **c.** She is at the office.
7. **a.** There's one behind this tall building. **b.** You can buy milk and bread there. **c.** Where is the nearest supermarket?

Conversation

Track 30

Listen to each conversation and answer the question.

1. **a.** keep walking down the road **b.** take a left **c.** go back
2. **a.** on the second floor **b.** in the basement **c.** outside of the house
3. **a.** something to wear around his neck **b.** something to wear on his hands **c.** something to wear on his head

Reading Questions

Vocabulary and Grammar

Choose the best answer to fill in each blank.

1. We live on the top ________________ of the building.
   a. house **b.** section **c.** floor **d.** basement

2. I really need to study hard. My English is ________________!
   a. popular **b.** terrible **c.** broken **d.** excellent

3. She climbs the ________________ to get to her office. It saves energy.
   a. departments **b.** stairs **c.** courts **d.** shops

4. We should ask the man for ________________ to our hotel.
   a. direction **b.** direct **c.** directions **d.** directors

5. ________________ to be more quiet.
   a. Please to try **b.** Please trying **c.** Please try **d.** Please

6. Never ________________ hiking by yourself. It's dangerous.
   a. goes **b.** going **c.** go **d.** to go

7. ________________ touch this hot stove! It can burn you.
   a. Does not **b.** Do not **c.** Not **d.** Please not

Cloze

Choose the best answer to fill in each blank.

The biggest department store in the world is in Centum City, South Korea. It is called Shinsegae Centum City and is 14 **1.** ________________ tall. The second biggest is the Macy's store in New York, and it is only half Shinsegae's size. More than 6,000 people work at Shinsegae, and it has many activities inside. There is a golf **2.** ________________, a spa, a place to ice-skate, and even an area to buy art. It has a theater restaurant called Cine de Chef. It serves food and **3.** ________________ movies. Shinsegae means "new world" in Korean, and Shinsegae Centum City is like a whole world inside a department store.

1. **a.** stairs **b.** stories **c.** buildings **d.** meters
2. **a.** playground **b.** pool **c.** course **d.** field
3. **a.** produces **b.** shows **c.** watches **d.** shoots

UNIT 7

Daily Life

Words

Track 31

Listen to the audio. Match the pictures with the words or phrases you hear.

1.

a 

b 

c 

2.

a 

b 

c 

Conversation

A. Complete the Dialogue

Choose the answers.

1. A: ____________________ B: Sure. How can I help you?
   a. Where are you going? **b.** How about you? **c.** Can you do me a favor?

2. A: ____________________ I have to put gas in my car. **B:** There is an ATM in the department store.
   a. Can you watch my little sister? **b.** Can I borrow $20? **c.** Can you help me with my homework?

3. A: I don't have enough gas to go there. **B:** OK. Here's $20. ____________________
   a. I have to pick up my clothes. **b.** I can stay until six o'clock. **c.** I'm happy to help.

B. Comprehension

Track 32

Listen to the dialogue. Choose the answers.

1. What is Debby doing?
   a. She is watching TV. **b.** She is visiting a sick friend.
   c. She is sending a package. **d.** She is doing the dishes.

2. Where is Tom's brother?
   a. He is at school. **b.** He is at home.
   c. He is at the library. **d.** He is at the hospital.

Grammar

Choose the answers.

1. ________________ I driving too fast?
   a. Are **b.** Am **c.** Is **d.** How
2. The bus driver ________________ on his cell phone.
   a. is talk **b.** not talking **c.** are talking **d.** is talking
3. Bill's parents are ________________ in Europe.
   a. not work **b.** works **c.** work **d.** working
4. Julia and her sister ________________ in the pool.
   a. is swimming **b.** are swimming **c.** swimming **d.** swims
5. Is anything wrong? ________________ is your father running?
   a. What **b.** Who **c.** Why **d.** How

Reading

A. Fill in the Blanks

Use the correct form of the words to complete the sentences.

training	class	fly	engine	swimming

1. Craig is taking a lot of ________________ in university.
2. All new workers receive ________________.
3. Jim can fix car ________________. He works in a garage.
4. It takes a long time to learn to ________________ an airplane.
5. My father is a(n) ________________ coach.

B. Comprehension Track 33

Listen to the article. Choose the answers.

1. What kind of training do astronauts go through first?
   a. flight training **b.** long training **c.** everyday training **d.** basic training
2. When do astronauts have to pass a swimming test?
   a. in the first month **b.** in 15 hours **c.** after 18 months **d.** in the first week
3. What does walking in the pool feel like?
   a. swimming in air **b.** flying in space **c.** flying an airplane **d.** running every day

Listening Questions

Best Response Questions

Track 34

Listen to the question or statement and choose the best response.

1. **a.** I take a bus. It's the quickest way. **b.** I usually play video games. **c.** I study between classes.
2. **a.** No. I'm just watching TV. **b.** Yes. Let's go watch a movie. **c.** No. I have to go to the post office.
3. **a.** My roommate and I study together. **b.** I study at the school library. **c.** I prefer to study at night.
4. **a.** Let's find you a good job. **b.** OK. There's an ATM over there. **c.** I'm very rich.
5. **a.** Can your dog do tricks? **b.** Sure. I'm happy to help. **c.** My watch says five p.m.
6. **a.** Most days, I ride a scooter. **b.** I always leave at about 8:00. **c.** I have classes from Monday to Friday.
7. **a.** I seldom clean it. **b.** Here is the mop. **c.** That's a dirty floor.

Conversation

Track 35

Listen to each conversation and answer the question.

1. **a.** put the dishes on the table **b.** wash the plates and bowls **c.** make some new dishes
2. **a.** He wants the woman to leave. **b.** He wants the woman to talk to him. **c.** He wants to talk to his brother.
3. **a.** during the movie **b.** after the movie **c.** before the movie

Reading Questions

Vocabulary and Grammar

Choose the best answer to fill in each blank.

1. You can't wash the shirt in a machine. You have to take it to the ________________.
   a. dry cleaners **b.** library **c.** gas station **d.** post office

2. He needs to go to the ________________ to buy some eye medicine.
   a. hospital **b.** drugstore **c.** garage **d.** dentist

3. Joyce is almost ________________ reading the novel.
   a. finishes **b.** to finish **c.** finished **d.** finishing

4. Is there ________________ in the office today?
   a. no one **b.** anyone **c.** some people **d.** everyone

5. ________________ the kids ________________ lunch at the hot dog place?
   a. Does, having **b.** Doing, have **c.** Are, have **d.** Are, having

6. Tim is sick, so he ________________ in bed.
   a. lay **b.** lie **c.** lying **d.** is lying

7. **A:** ________________ is he talking about?
   B: He's telling Jack about his car.
   a. What **b.** Who **c.** Why **d.** When

Cloze

Choose the best answer to fill in each blank.

Astronauts need a lot of training. They need to be good in school and also very healthy. First, they have to take **1.** ________________ training. This training takes 18 months. The students have classes every day, so they spend a lot of time **2.** ________________. They learn how to fly **3.** ________________ and spend 15 hours a week in the air. They also need to know how to use a space station's computers. A lot of the training happens under the water. While in the water, they have to wear shoes and clothes. This helps them prepare for moving and walking in space.

1. **a.** many **b.** deep **c.** low **d.** basic

2. **a.** exercising **b.** studying **c.** traveling **d.** fixing

3. **a.** engines **b.** programs **c.** airplanes **d.** balloons

UNIT 8

Out in Nature

Words

Track 36

Listen to the audio. Match the pictures with the words you hear.

1.

a

b

c

2.

a

b

c

Conversation

A. Matching

Match the sentences.

a. No, you don't. I know my way around.	**b.** Not really. People respect nature.
c. It's very peaceful.	**d.** Cool. I can't wait.

1. **A:** What's it like around there? **B:** ____________________
2. **A:** I don't have to work tomorrow. We should go hiking. **B:** ____________________
3. **A:** Do I need a good map? **B:** ____________________
4. **A:** Is there much pollution? **B:** ____________________

B. Comprehension

Track 37

Listen to the dialogue. Check ***True*** *or* ***False****.*

	True	False
1. Karen wants to find her lunch before she leaves the station.	☐	☐
2. Karen goes to this area all the time.	☐	☐
3. There are really big forests and many green fields in the countryside.	☐	☐
4. People care about nature around there.	☐	☐
5. Pollution is a serious problem in that area.	☐	☐

Unit Test

Grammar

Choose the correct words.

1. I'm happy here because / until the countryside is so beautiful.
2. Julia can watch TV although / after she does the dishes.
3. I want to call my mother because / before we leave.
4. Though / When Tony is smart, he doesn't get good grades.
5. Let's play cards since / until the bus gets here.
6. I can read a magazine while / so I wait for you.

Reading

A. Fill in the Blanks

Use the correct form of the words to complete the sentences.

high	sky	pass	depend	serious

1. Noise pollution is a ________________ problem in big cities.
2. The Amazon River ________________ through a huge rain forest.
3. There are dark clouds in the ________________.
4. Tom ________________ on his family for money.
5. Mount Everest is almost nine kilometers ________________.

B. Comprehension Track 38

*Listen to the article. Check **True** or **False**.*

	True	False
1. Victoria Falls is in Africa.	☐	☐
2. It is best to see Victoria Falls from the ground.	☐	☐
3. The Nile has three main tributaries.	☐	☐
4. Lake Baikal is the oldest lake in the world.	☐	☐
5. There is no pollution in Lake Baikal.	☐	☐

Listening Questions

Best Response Questions

Track 39

Listen to the question or statement and choose the best response.

1. **a.** Yes. I like waterfalls. **b.** Sure. I enjoy swimming. **c.** Where are you going?
2. **a.** No. I live on a small street. **b.** No. I live on a small island. **c.** No. I prefer to live near a lake.
3. **a.** No. I like the mountains. **b.** I like cities better. **c.** I love doing that.
4. **a.** No. It's very boring. **b.** Yes. It's easy to ride a bike there. **c.** Yes. There are mountains everywhere.
5. **a.** I like to hike in the woods. **b.** I want to go fishing in the sea. **c.** I usually go to a forest on my boat.
6. **a.** There is a lot of corn here! **b.** I know. The trees are really tall. **c.** Yes. The water is so nice.
7. **a.** Alright. We can go camping there. **b.** I don't go very often. **c.** Great! I want to go shopping.

Conversation

Track 40

Listen to each conversation and answer the question.

1. **a.** The wind is quite strong there. **b.** The air is clean there. **c.** It's really small.
2. **a.** They're very big. **b.** They have a nice color. **c.** He likes to drink coffee.
3. **a.** It is close to their house. **b.** It is quiet. **c.** It is exciting.

Reading Questions

Vocabulary and Grammar

Choose the best answer to fill in each blank.

1. England is on the other side of the ________________ from America.
   a. desert **b.** ocean **c.** river **d.** valley

2. After a long hike, I love to wash myself under the ________________.
   a. beach **b.** field **c.** waterfall **d.** island

3. I can't wait ________________ to the forest. I love nature.
   a. for going **b.** to going **c.** but go **d.** to go

4. What is Paris like? Can you ________________ it?
   a. describe **b.** talk **c.** respect **d.** record

5. Let's eat dinner ________________ we leave.
   a. when **b.** until **c.** before **d.** since

6. You shouldn't go running right now ________________ it is raining.
   a. after **b.** though **c.** because **d.** so

7. ________________ hamburgers are delicious, eating too many is not good for you.
   a. If **b.** Although **c.** However **d.** When

Cloze

Choose the best answer to fill in each blank.

There are many wonderful places in the world. Victoria Falls is a waterfall in Africa. It is the largest one in the world. At 108 meters, it's also quite high. The Nile is the longest river. It runs through Egypt. The people there use its water for their fields. Lots of people **1.** ________________ on it to live. There are many stories about this river. It's a very popular place to visit. Lake Baikal is the deepest and biggest freshwater lake on earth. It's 25 million years old, so it's also the **2.** ________________ lake. The lake is beautiful and peaceful, but it is in danger because of **3.** ________________.

1. **a.** reply **b.** depend **c.** build **d.** pass
2. **a.** oldest **b.** dirtiest **c.** greatest **d.** most famous
3. **a.** polluted **b.** pollution **c.** polluting **d.** pollute

UNIT 9

On Campus

Words Track 41

Listen and match the audio with the words or phrases.

1. a report | b pass | c final exam

2. a fail | b semester | c review

Conversation

A. Complete the Dialogue

Choose the answers.

1. **A:** Look at the results of my final exams. I failed all of them. **B:** ________________ I'm too lazy.
   a. Did you get bad grades? **b.** I'm not so good. **c.** I didn't do well either.

2. **A:** We need to improve our study skills. **B:** You're right. ________________
   a. Did you also get low grades last time? **b.** How do you study for your exams? **c.** Why don't you stop reading the books?

3. **A:** I usually start studying the day before the test. **B:** ________________
   a. You have terrible study habits too! **b.** Something bad happened. **c.** I did! It was too difficult.

B. Comprehension Track 42

Listen to the dialogue. Choose the answers.

1. How did Simon do on the exam?
   a. He got a good grade. **b.** He didn't pass.
   c. He got 100 percent **d.** He didn't take the exam at all.

2. When did Simon start to read the book?
   a. one day before the exam **b.** one week before the exam
   c. the day after the exam **d.** on the weekend before the exam

3. Why didn't Mark get a good grade either?
   a. He had to help one of his friends. **b.** The teacher doesn't like him.
   c. He read the wrong book for the exam. **d.** He didn't prepare enough.

Grammar

Write questions in the simple past for the following answers.

1. Yes, I got a good grade on my report. → ____________________
2. No, Alice wasn't very sad. → ____________________
3. Yes, my brother played baseball yesterday. → ____________________
4. Yes, I ate lunch. → ____________________
5. Yes, they were hungry. → ____________________
6. No, he didn't read the letter. → ____________________

Reading

A. Fill in the Blanks

Use the correct form of the words to complete the sentences.

live	grow	choose	rent	online

1. The ____________ for my apartment is $550 a month.
2. I am taking two ____________ courses this semester.
3. Sales of our new product ____________ a lot last month.
4. My brother and I ____________ to go to different universities.
5. Julia doesn't want to ____________ on campus.

B. Comprehension Track 43

Listen to the article. Choose the answers.

1. More and more students ____________ these days.
   a. leave their town **b.** rent an apartment
   c. have parties **d.** study online

2. Why are online classes so popular today?
   a. They are easier to complete. **b.** They are cheaper.
   c. They are quieter. **d.** They are more fun.

3. When do students get the best results?
   a. when they study in their bedroom only **b.** when they study online and in a classroom
   c. when they study online and stay home **d.** when they study in a classroom with a good teacher

Listening Questions

Best Response Questions

Track 44

Listen to the question or statement and choose the best response.

1. **a.** History is my favorite subject. **b.** I'm good at singing. **c.** I always do well in my science courses.
2. **a.** Not really. It's easy to pass. **b.** Yes, I usually pass. **c.** Yes, our teacher is nice.
3. **a.** I have more work to do later. **b.** They're fine. I always get A's. **c.** I study hard before my exams.
4. **a.** I like my college the best. **b.** I get good grades. **c.** I can study my favorite subjects.
5. **a.** I had a cup of coffee and cookie. **b.** A few people had a fight in class. **c.** We planned a party for our a history teacher.
6. **a.** No. I prefer math to history. **b.** Yes. I have a lot of schoolwork to do every night. **c.** No. I don't really enjoy it.
7. **a.** Yes, he's my best friend. **b.** Yes. He always studies. **c.** Yes. He doesn't like to study.

Conversation

Track 45

Listen to each conversation and answer the question.

1. **a.** The woman is smart. **b.** He trusts the woman. **c.** The woman often has good ideas.
2. **a.** The man found a good job. **b.** The woman got her test scores. **c.** The woman had a test.
3. **a.** It was always good. **b.** It was really funny. **c.** It became much better.

Reading Questions

Vocabulary and Grammar

Choose the best answer to fill in each blank.

1. He is taking a history ________________ in school.

   a. course　　b. report　　c. skill　　d. semester

2. Study hard so you can ________________ the test.

   a. choose　　b. review　　c. fail　　d. pass

3. Chris doesn't really like the book. I don't ________________.

   a. either　　b. too　　c. neither　　d. also

4. My parents ________________ very happy when I broke the washing machine.

   a. weren't　　b. wasn't　　c. didn't　　d. isn't

5. I ________________ to the clothes store yesterday, and I ________________ two coats.

   a. go, buy　　b. go, brought　　c. went, bought　　d. went, buying

6. A: Why did he ________________ his job?
   B: He ________________ a new job with higher pay.

   a. left, did find　　b. leaves, found　　c. leave, found　　d. leave, finds

7. I ________________ that book last week.

   a. read　　b. to read　　c. reads　　d. reading

Cloze

Choose the best answer to fill in each blank.

For most people, college means leaving home, living somewhere else, and going to class. Some people, however, don't have to do these things. They study online. In the U.S., more than five million students study through the Internet. 30 percent of new students choose to do it these days. Online classes are popular because students don't have to go to the **1.** ________________ to study. They can study at their homes. Around 66 percent of American universities **2.** ________________ online courses. Also, online courses are less **3.** ________________ because students don't have to find an apartment to live near the university. More and more students are choosing to study online every year.

1. a. website　　b. bedroom　　c. computer　　d. campus

2. a. accept　　b. offer　　c. prepare　　d. improve

3. a. cheaper　　b. interesting　　c. expensive　　d. more

UNIT 10 Happy Times

Words

Track 46

Listen to the audio. Match the pictures with the words you hear.

1\.

a

b

c

2\.

a

b

c

Conversation

A. Matching

Match the sentences.

a. Oh! Then I have to clean my suit.
b. It's on Friday, October 11th.
c. I'd love to. What should I wear?
d. At six o'clock. The dinner starts at six thirty.

1. **A:** Would you like to attend my sister's wedding with me? **B:** ____________________
2. **A:** When do we need to arrive? **B:** ____________________
3. **A:** When is the meeting? **B:** ____________________
4. **A:** It's a formal party. **B:** ____________________

B. Comprehension

Track 47

*Listen to the dialogue. Check **True** or **False**.*

	True	False
1. Glenn is having a birthday party for his brother.	☐	☐
2. The guests have to arrive before 11:30 in the morning.	☐	☐
3. Glenn hired a jazz band to play at the party.	☐	☐
4. Guys and girls have to dress nicely for the party.	☐	☐
5. Judy can see Glenn's cousin on the big day.	☐	☐

Grammar

Choose the answers.

1. Doug doesn't drink coffee ________ night.
   a. in **b.** on **c.** at **d.** before

2. My birthday is ________ July ninth.
   a. for **b.** in **c.** at **d.** on

3. The movie starts ________ eight o'clock.
   a. at **b.** on **c.** during **d.** in

4. Carl went to Thailand ________ last month.
   a. on **b.** in **c.** at **d.** X

5. It gets nice and cool ________ evening.
   a. in **b.** in the **c.** on the **d.** at

Reading

A. Fill in the Blanks

Use the correct form of the words to complete the sentences.

happen	event	host	cheer	during

1. It rains a lot ________ spring.
2. South Korea ________ the Summer Olympics in 1988.
3. All the students came to ________ for their school team.
4. The U.S. Open is a very exciting sports ________.
5. The incident ________ after midnight.

B. Comprehension Track 48

*Listen to the article. Check **True** or **False**.*

	True	False
1. The FIFA World Cup finals last for one month.	☐	☐
2. Every country in the world is in the FIFA World Cup finals.	☐	☐
3. The FIFA World Cup happens every two years in the summer.	☐	☐
4. The FIFA World Cup host countries get lots of visitors.	☐	☐
5. Lots of people have World Cup parties with their friends.	☐	☐

Listening Questions

Best Response Questions

Track 49

Listen to the question or statement and choose the best response.

1. **a.** Best wishes to your family. **b.** It was a good time. **c.** That sounds fun.
2. **a.** I like to eat at this restaurant. **b.** I don't really like music. **c.** I love Christmas parties.
3. **a.** I didn't read it. **b.** Yes. They're for the 25th. **c.** I like books about trains.
4. **a.** I just want to go shopping. **b.** I got here last week. **c.** I don't live near here.
5. **a.** We can take her to her favorite restaurant. **b.** Yes, let's do that. **c.** Happy birthday.
6. **a.** I decorate my house. **b.** Thanks. I'd love to. **c.** I prefer to get money.
7. **a.** Yes. I can't wait. It should be fun. **b.** I think it's in a big hotel. **c.** No. The tickets are too expensive.

Conversation

Track 50

Listen to each conversation and answer the question.

1. **a.** books **b.** clothes **c.** food
2. **a.** an old friend of the man's **b.** the man's college classmate **c.** a person in the man's family
3. **a.** She can wear her usual clothes. **b.** She should wear formal clothes. **c.** She should wear a dress.

Reading Questions

Vocabulary and Grammar

Choose the best answer to fill in each blank.

1. He ________________ them into his house.
   a. welcomed b. entered c. invited d. spent

2. Her parents gave her a new computer as a ________________.
   a. price b. present c. prize d. purpose

3. We should ________________ for the dinner party.
   a. dress out b. dress up as c. dress down d. dress up

4. I can bring a ________________ to the ball game. Do you want to come with me?
   a. guess b. parent c. guest d. child

5. She works at a restaurant ________________ 8:00 a.m. and 11:00 a.m.
   a. on b. from c. before d. between

6. Winter comes ________________ spring.
   a. before b. after c. in d. at

7. The sales meeting is ________________ next Thursday.
   a. for b. in c. at d. X

Cloze

Choose the best answer to fill in each blank.

The world's biggest party is the FIFA World Cup. Every four years, every country comes together to celebrate the World Cup finals for a(n) **1.** ________________ month. It is the biggest sports event in the world. There are 32 teams in the World Cup finals, and they are each from a different country. Many countries want to host the World Cup finals because they bring in many **2.** ________________. People go to the finals to attend the games, have parties, and **3.** ________________. Not everyone can travel a long distance to see the World Cup, so many people hold parties at their homes or at bars. This way, everyone can celebrate the World Cup.

1. a. total b. active c. half of the d. whole

2. a. visitors b. success c. money d. presidents

3. a. play b. take part c. win d. cheer

UNIT 11 Food to Go

Words

Track 51

Listen to the audio. Match the pictures with the words you hear.

1\. a  b  c 

2\. a  b  c 

Conversation

A. Matching

Match the sentences.

a. Let me see. The total comes to $9.50.	**b.** Sure. We have soda and juice.
c. It's just around the corner.	**d.** I would like a small cup of coffee, please.

1. **A:** Where is the clothing store? **B:** ____________
2. **A:** How much does everything cost? **B:** ____________
3. **A:** Hello. Can I take your order? **B:** ____________
4. **A:** I want to get a drink. **B:** ____________

B. Comprehension

Track 52

Listen to the dialogue. Check ***True*** *or* ***False****.*

	True	False
1. Sam wants to eat a lot of food.	☐	☐
2. Marcy gets a medium strawberry shake.	☐	☐
3. Marcy thinks Sam looks thin.	☐	☐
4. Marcy orders one egg sandwich, one soda, and one shake.	☐	☐
5. The waitress needs five minutes to finish the order.	☐	☐

Grammar

Choose the answers.

1. Megan just got back from vacation. She looks ________________.
   a. wonder b. wonderful c. wonderfully d. wondered

2. Do you see the ________________ bright light?
   a. quiet b. two c. a d. really

3. It's ________________ outside. Why are you bringing a scarf?
   a. cold b. hungry c. warm d. lovely

4. Which sentence is CORRECT?
   a. She's very fast at it. b. This is a really restaurant.
   c. I ate a quickly meal. d. I would like a drink large.

5. Laura and Adam's wedding is on Sunday. They're ________________ about it.
   a. exciting b. excited c. excite d. excites

Reading

A. Fill in the Blanks

Use the correct form of the words to complete the sentences.

effect	menu	tired	energy	worried

1. This restaurant has a big ________________. There are lots of things to choose from.
2. Peter didn't have enough ________________ to go running.
3. What ________________ does coffee have on you?
4. Laura's parents were ________________ about her grades.
5. If you're feeling ________________, try taking a nap.

B. Comprehension Track 53

Listen to the article. Check ***True*** *or* ***False****.*

	True	False
1. Morgan Spurlock made a movie to show good effects of fast food.	☐	☐
2. The book *Super Size Me* is about fast food around the world.	☐	☐
3. Morgan Spurlock ate at McDonald's for an entire month.	☐	☐
4. Doctors were worried about Morgan Spurlock's heart.	☐	☐
5. Morgan Spurlock was able to lose 11 kilograms in one month.	☐	☐

Listening Questions

Best Response Questions

Track 54

Listen to the question or statement and choose the best response.

1. **a.** Sorry. I can get you a new one. **b.** Here's your change. **c.** Good. I'm glad to help.
2. **a.** Here's your tea. **b.** That's a lot of juice. **c.** The total is $4.50.
3. **a.** No. This doesn't taste good. **b.** No. I don't like to eat fast food. **c.** I eat at this restaurant sometimes.
4. **a.** Yes, I want to order. **b.** What would you like to order? **c.** No. Your order is not ready yet.
5. **a.** Sure. I would like everything on it. **b.** No problem. I can help you. **c.** No. That's everything. Thank you.
6. **a.** What do you need? **b.** Yes, but it costs a little more money. **c.** No, we don't have that here.
7. **a.** You don't have to pay. **b.** Sorry. I need another minute. **c.** Yes, this is my order.

Conversation

Track 55

Listen to each conversation and answer the question.

1. **a.** make a call **b.** go outside **c.** sit down
2. **a.** It's very near. **b.** They need to take the train. **c.** It's on the corner of two streets.
3. **a.** She is nice to talk to. **b.** She is a teacher in the school. **c.** She is happy right now.

Reading Questions

Vocabulary and Grammar

Choose the best answer to fill in each blank.

1. Amy likes ________________ salt on her food.
   a. extra　**b.** super　**c.** large　**d.** few

2. We need some fresh tomatoes to make ________________.
   a. fries　**b.** soda　**c.** shakes　**d.** ketchup

3. Do you have ________________ for $100?
   a. bills　**b.** money　**c.** change　**d.** coins

4. This drink is too big. Can I change it for a(n) ________________ size instead?
   a. larger　**b.** another　**c.** same　**d.** medium

5. ________________ mother teaches me how to be a good person.
   a. This　**b.** My　**c.** The　**d.** One

6. She is really ________________ with her new job.
   a. please　**b.** pleases　**c.** pleasing　**d.** pleased

7. Thank you for dinner. I had a ________________ time.
   a. likely　**b.** lonely　**c.** lovely　**d.** luckily

Cloze

Choose the best answer to fill in each blank.

Everyone knows that too much fast food is not good for you. However, millions of people eat it many times a week. In 2003, Morgan Spurlock decided to eat at McDonald's three times a day for a month. He shot a movie about it and called it *Super Size Me*. It shows the terrible **1.** ________________ of fast food on a person's health. Spurlock tried everything on the menu. He started having health problems. He often felt **2.** ________________. He also had trouble with his heart. He **3.** ________________ more than 11 kilograms that month. It took him over a year to go back to his regular weight. Spurlock's movie tells people about the dangers of fast food.

1. **a.** affects　**b.** reasons　**c.** problems　**d.** effects
2. **a.** alone　**b.** clever　**c.** tired　**d.** full
3. **a.** gained　**b.** added　**c.** rose　**d.** lost

UNIT 12

On the Road

Words Track 56

Listen and match the audio with the words or phrases.

1. a tour group | b tour guide | c abroad

2. a ski | b visit | c postcard

Conversation

A. Matching

Match the sentences.

a. Great. He must know lots of good places to visit.
b. I'm going to go to Thailand.
c. I know. You're an independent person.
d. Yeah. That is a wonderful city.

1. **A:** Do you have any plans for the summer? **B:** ______
2. **A:** I don't like group travel. I usually make plans as I go. **B:** ______
3. **A:** My friend is a tour guide. **B:** ______
4. **A:** All my friends love Beijing. **B:** ______

B. Comprehension Track 57

*Listen to the dialogue. Check **True** or **False**.*

	True	False
1. Ted is looking for work.	☐	☐
2. Ted likes the Philippines.	☐	☐
3. Will likes to travel by himself.	☐	☐
4. Ted knows a tour guide in the Philippines.	☐	☐
5. Will is picking apples in the Philippines.	☐	☐

Grammar

Choose the answers.

1. Sam ________________ going to ________________ his homework.
   a. is, done b. is, do c. was, doing d. was, did

2. A: Are you going to leave your job? B: ________________
   a. No, you are. b. No, I am. c. Yes, you are. d. Yes, I am.

3. Which sentence uses the future tense?
   a. Nancy Anderson plays the piano well.
   b. The baby is crying loudly. I want to hold her.
   c. Steven and his friends are going to the movies.
   d. James is talking about his plans for next year.

4. I am ________________ a book.
   a. read b. going reading c. be going to read d. going to read

5. Chris is ________________ French in Paris.
   a. going studying b. studies c. study d. going to study

Reading

A. Fill in the Blanks

Use the correct form of the words to complete the sentences.

unique	space	island	rise	seat

1. A(n) ________________ has water all around it.
2. That ring is so ________________. It's really one of a kind.
3. Grandpa got out of bed before the sun ________________ this morning.
4. This is a large bus. We can easily find ________________.
5. Yuri Gagarin was the first man to travel into ________________.

B. Comprehension Track 58

*Listen to the article. Check **True** or **False**.*

	True	False
1. Training takes three days to complete.	☐	☐
2. It's difficult to see the Earth from the space hotel.	☐	☐
3. The space hotel guests can watch the sun rise several times a day.	☐	☐
4. Each spaceship can fit 40,000 people.	☐	☐
5. It costs three million dollars for a trip to space.	☐	☐

Listening Questions

Best Response Questions

Track 59

Listen to the question or statement and choose the best response.

1. **a.** I prefer going to the countryside. **b.** I enjoy traveling by myself. **c.** I often take the train.
2. **a.** No. I'm not going to bring my camera. **b.** Yes. I'm going to visit Canada next month. **c.** I plan to go by airplane.
3. **a.** No. She usually goes with a tour group. **b.** Not really. She's very independent. **c.** Yes. She's going to leave on Wednesday.
4. **a.** I love driving my car. **b.** You can learn a lot when you travel. **c.** I want to go to Europe.
5. **a.** I usually bring a few novels to read. **b.** The postcards look beautiful. **c.** I'm too scared to fly.
6. **a.** I go to Japan often. **b.** I would like to visit Spain. **c.** I like to spend time with my family.
7. **a.** Yes. He's learning to drive. **b.** Yes. I hope he passes! **c.** No. He's still there.

Conversation

Track 60

Listen to each conversation and answer the question.

1. **a.** It was excellent. **b.** It made him cry. **c.** It bored him.
2. **a.** see the islands **b.** buy an island **c.** stay in a lot of hotels
3. **a.** Joe didn't call him. **b.** Joe was not honest with him. **c.** Joe made fun of him.

Reading Questions

Vocabulary and Grammar

Choose the best answer to fill in each blank.

1. Don't forget to buy us some presents while you are on ________________.
   a. vacation **b.** trip **c.** visit **d.** tour

2. They hired a ________________ to show them around the city.
   a. user guide **b.** tour guide **c.** journalist **d.** professor

3. He moved to Australia for one year to study ________________.
   a. aboard **b.** anywhere **c.** board **d.** abroad

4. Is Mike here ________________? I need to talk to him.
   a. well **b.** just **c.** yet **d.** until

5. A few of my friends ________________ skiing later this afternoon.
   a. is going **b.** are going to **c.** go **d.** are going

6. We're ________________ London at the end of the month.
   a. going to fly to **b.** went to **c.** go to **d.** flying

7. **A:** ________________ are they going to eat?
   B: They want to try the new Thai restaurant.
   a. How **b.** Where **c.** When **d.** Which

Cloze

Choose the best answer to fill in each blank.

If you want to go on a trip to space, you have to prepare for 16 weeks. In the future, you may be able to travel to outer space and stay there for three days. One company is building a space hotel. After you take the training on an island, you **1.** ________________ a spaceship up to the hotel and watch the **2.** ________________ from 450 kilometers above the ground. These trips are **3.** ________________, so not too many people can pay for them now. Soon, however, space travel may cost less, and even common people may be able to go to space.

1. **a.** tour **b.** ride **c.** travel **d.** fly
2. **a.** sky **b.** moon **c.** space **d.** earth
3. **a.** expensive **b.** unique **c.** effective **d.** private

Answer Key

UNIT 1 Just for Fun

Unit Test

Words

1. a 2. b

Conversation

A. Complete the Dialogue

1. b 2. a 3. b

B. Comprehension

1. c 2. a 3. b

Grammar

1. drives 2. do not/don't cook, eat
3. catches 4. studies 5. worry

Reading

A. Fill in the Blanks

1. active 2. hobbies 3. improve
4. interest 5. think

B. Comprehension

1. T 2. F 3. F 4. T 5. F

Listening Questions

Best Response Questions

1. b 2. c 3. c 4. c
5. a 6. c 7. a

Conversation

1. a 2. b 3. b

Reading Questions

Vocabulary and Grammar

1. c 2. b 3. a 4. d
5. c 6. c 7. d

Cloze

1. c 2. a 3. b

UNIT 2 Grocery Shpopping

Unit Test

Words

1. a 2. c

Conversation

A. Matching

1. d 2. c 3. b 4. a

B. Comprehension

1. F 2. T 3. T 4. F 5. F

Grammar

1. c 2. a 3. d 4. d
5. a 6. b

Reading

A. Fill in the Blanks

1. delicious 2. wedding 3. important
4. snack 5. meanings

B. Comprehension

1. T 2. F 3. F 4. T

Listening Questions

Best Response Questions

1. c 2. a 3. b 4. b
5. a 6. a 7. c

Conversation

1. b 2. c 3. a

Reading Questions

Vocabulary and Grammar

1. d 2. c 3. d 4. b
5. c 6. c 7. a

Cloze

1. b 2. d 3. d

UNIT 3 Blue Skies

Unit Test

Words

1. b **2.** c

Conversation

A. Complete the Dialogue

1. c **2.** c **3.** b

B. Comprehension

1. d **2.** b

Grammar

1. faster **2.** best **3.** friendlier/more friendly

4. quieter/more quiet **5.** coldest

Reading

A. Fill in the Blanks

1. dry **2.** speed **3.** low

4. sunny **5.** rain

B. Comprehension

1. F **2.** T **3.** T **4.** F **5.** F

Listening Questions

Best Response Questions

1. c **2.** b **3.** b **4.** a

5. c **6.** b **7.** b

Conversation

1. b **2.** c **3.** a

Reading Questions

Vocabulary and Grammar

1. d **2.** a **3.** a **4.** c

5. c **6.** a **7.** b

Cloze

1. c **2.** a **3.** b

UNIT 4 The World of Computers

Unit Test

Words

1. b **2.** c

Conversation

A. Matching

1. b **2.** d **3.** c **4.** a

B. Comprehension

1. F **2.** T **3.** T **4.** F **5.** T

Grammar

1. d **2.** b **3.** d **4.** c

Reading

A. Fill in the Blanks

1. access **2.** games **3.** smartphones

4. Internet **5.** train

B. Comprehension

1. a **2.** d **3.** a

Listening Questions

Best Response Questions

1. a **2.** b **3.** c **4.** b

5. b **6.** a **7.** b

Conversation

1. a **2.** b **3.** a

Reading Questions

Vocabulary and Grammar

1. a **2.** d **3.** b **4.** b

5. c **6.** d **7.** d

Cloze

1. d **2.** a **3.** d

Answer Key

UNIT 5 Man's Best Friends

Unit Test

Words

1. a 2. b

Conversation

A. Complete the Dialogue

1. b 2. b 3. c

B. Comprehension

1. a 2. a

Grammar

1. to have 2. to listen/listening
3. playing 4. Traveling
5. to finish 6. to buy

Reading

A. Fill in the Blanks

1. Wild 2. yard 3. understands
4. hippo 5. furniture

B. Comprehension

1. F 2. T 3. T 4. F 5. T

Listening Questions

Best Response Questions

1. b 2. a 3. c 4. a
5. c 6. c 7. a

Conversation

1. a 2. a 3. b

Reading Questions

Vocabulary and Grammar

1. d 2. c 3. c 4. b
5. d 6. d 7. c

Cloze

1. d 2. a 3. a

UNIT 6 At the Department Store

Unit Test

Words

1. c 2. a

Conversation

A. Matching

1. c 2. d 3. a 4. b

B. Comprehension

1. F 2. F 3. F 4. T 5. T

Grammar

1. d 2. b 3. a 4. b 5. c

Reading

A. Fill in the Blanks

1. serves 2. stories 3. ice-skate
4. means 5. space

B. Comprehension

1. F 2. F 3. T 4. F 5. F

Listening Questions

Best Response Questions

1. b 2. a 3. b 4. c
5. c 6. b 7. a

Conversation

1. a 2. a 3. b

Reading Questions

Vocabulary and Grammar

1. c 2. b 3. b 4. c
5. c 6. c 7. b

Cloze

1. b 2. c 3. b

UNIT 7 Daily Life

Unit Test

Words

1. c 2. b

Conversation

A. Complete the Dialogue

1. c 2. b 3. c

B. Comprehension

1. d 2. b

Grammar

1. b 2. d 3. d 4. b 5. c

Reading

A. Fill in the Blanks

1. classes 2. training 3. engines
4. fly 5. swimming

B. Comprehension

1. d 2. a 3. b

Listening Questions

Best Response Questions

1. b 2. a 3. c 4. b
5. b 6. a 7. a

Conversation

1. b 2. a 3. c

Reading Questions

Vocabulary and Grammar

1. a 2. b 3. c 4. b
5. d 6. d 7. a

Cloze

1. d 2. b 3. c

UNIT 8 Out in Nature

Unit Test

Words

1. c 2. a

Conversation

A. Matching

1. c 2. d 3. a 4. b

B. Comprehension

1. F 2. F 3. T 4. T 5. F

Grammar

1. because 2. after 3. before
4. Though 5. until 6. while

Reading

A. Fill in the Blanks

1. serious 2. passes 3. sky
4. depends 5. high

B. Comprehension

1. T 2. F 3. F 4. T 5. F

Listening Questions

Best Response Questions

1. b 2. b 3. b 4. b
5. b 6. a 7. a

Conversation

1. b 2. a 3. b

Reading Questions

Vocabulary and Grammar

1. b 2. c 3. d 4. a
5. c 6. c 7. b

Cloze

1. b 2. a 3. b

Answer Key

UNIT 9 On Campus

Unit Test

Words

1. c 2. c

Conversation

A. Complete the Dialogue

1. c 2. b 3. a

B. Comprehension

1. b 2. a 3. d

Grammar

1. Did you get a good grade on your report?
2. Was Alice very sad?
3. Did your brother play baseball yesterday?
4. Did you eat lunch?
5. Were they hungry?
6. Did he read the letter?

Reading

A. Fill in the Blanks

1. rent 2. online 3. grew
4. chose 5. live

B. Comprehension

1. d 2. b 3. d

Listening Questions

Best Response Questions

1. c 2. a 3. b 4. c
5. b 6. b 7. c

Conversation

1. b 2. b 3. c

Reading Questions

Vocabulary and Grammar

1. a 2. d 3. a 4. a
5. c 6. c 7. a

Cloze

1. d 2. b 3. c

UNIT 10 Happy Times

Unit Test

Words

1. a 2. b

Conversation

A. Matching

1. c 2. d 3. b 4. a

B. Comprehension

1. F 2. T 3. T 4. T 5. F

Grammar

1. c 2. d 3. a 4. d 5. b

Reading

A. Fill in the Blanks

1. during 2. hosted 3. cheer
4. event 5. happened

B. Comprehension

1. T 2. F 3. F 4. T 5. T

Listening Questions

Best Response Questions

1. c 2. b 3. b 4. b
5. a 6. a 7. a

Conversation

1. b 2. c 3. a

Reading Questions

Vocabulary and Grammar

1. a 2. b 3. d 4. c
5. d 6. a 7. d

Cloze

1. d 2. a 3. d

UNIT 11 Food to Go

Unit Test

Words

1. c 2. a

Conversation

A. Complete the Dialogue

1. c 2. a 3. d 4. b

B. Comprehension

1. T 2. F 3. F 4. F 5. T

Grammar

1. b 2. d 3. c 4. a 5. b

Reading

A. Fill in the Blanks

1. menu 2. energy 3. effects
4. worried 5. tired

B. Comprehension

1. F 2. F 3. T 4. T 5. F

Listening Questions

Best Response Questions

1. a 2. c 3. b 4. c
5. c 6. b 7. b

Conversation

1. c 2. a 3. a

Reading Questions

Vocabulary and Grammar

1. a 2. d 3. c 4. d
5. b 6. d 7. c

Cloze

1. d 2. c 3. a

UNIT 12 On the Road

Unit Test

Words

1. a 2. a

Conversation

A. Matching

1. b 2. c 3. a 4. d

B. Comprehension

1. T 2. T 3. T 4. F 5. F

Grammar

1. b 2. d 3. c 4. d 5. d

Reading

A. Fill in the Blanks

1. island 2. unique 3. rose
4. seats 5. space

B. Comprehension

1. F 2. F 3. T 4. F 5. T

Listening Questions

Best Response Questions

1. b 2. b 3. a 4. a
5. a 6. b 7. b

Conversation

1. a 2. a 3. a

Reading Questions

Vocabulary and Grammar

1. a 2. b 3. d 4. c
5. d 6. a 7. b

Cloze

1. b 2. d 3. a